The Knot

THE
KNOT

Winner of the
Beatrice Hawley
Award

Alice Jones

alicejamesbooks

Cambridge, Massachusetts

ACKNOWLEDGMENTS

Thanks to Brenda Hillman, Bob Hass, and Jeanne Foster for their comments on the manuscript and to Tom Ogden, whose thoughts on an autistic/contiguous phase crept into some poems.

I would like to thank the editors of the following magazines where some of the poems, or earlier versions of them, appeared:

Cream City Review: "Anorexia" and "The Pool"
The Gettysburg Review: "Balance Point" and "Undertow"
New England Review: "The Cadaver"
Poetry: "Persephone," "Brother and Sister" and "Prayer"
ZYZZYVA: "The Biopsy"

Alice James Books gratefully acknowledges support from the National Endowment for the Arts and from the Massachusetts Council on the Arts and Humanities, a state agency whose funds are recommended by the Governor and appropriated by the State Legislature.

Alice James Books are published by the Alice James Poetry Cooperative, Inc.
Alice James Books, 33 Richdale Avenue, Cambridge, Massachusetts 02140.

For my mother

Contents

ONE

Peter Stefan Devyatkin
3/30/51–8/18/91

The Umbrella

Since they wouldn't let him out
of bed, I did his Christmas
shopping for him—a Matisse
calendar for his mother, *Puss
in Boots* for his son. But I wanted
one gift. So after the goodbye
kiss, holding his damp face
in my hands, hoping the bitterness
in my eyes would not spill,

I said—it's raining outside
and I don't have one. I wanted
some part of him to take with me,
something more solid than
the visual memories—the postcard
he sent of Artaud in *St. Joan*,
a stolen copy of *The Celtic
Twilight*, *Children of Paradise*
seen two times through.

He said—it's a good one, was,
from Brooks Brothers, found
abandoned in the library at work,
it's old, mended a couple of times,
but it keeps you dry.

Once, I had wished him dead.
I saw in his pale eyes my wish
coming true. Then we nodded
in the old way, sharing one thought—
me walking out, sheltered, into
the drizzly December afternoon,
going on; Peter staying here
at St. Vincent's, never going out
again under the liquid sky.

In the Pine Woods

He'd eat rare hamburgers with
ketchup, I'd have one snowy scoop
of cottage cheese on a rumpled bed
of iceberg lettuce, then he'd go off
to his Polar Explorations class and
I'd walk west, out to the grove of
Christmas trees. Among the waist-high,
bottle-brush shrubs, the buttercups
and purple clover, I'd spread out
one of the India prints, strip, lie
naked in the afternoon sun, unseen
among the resinous, growing trees,

while he learned about lost expeditions—
one leader gone mad; one former
Cincinnatian dug up in Greenland
on the hundredth anniversary
of his death, searching for a route
to the Pole, found poisoned with
arsenic; crews lost in the north woods,
or stranded on ice floes, suspected
cannibals, all contending to be
first to arrive in virgin territory.

I'd look down at the pale mounds
of my shrinking self, wanting
a biscuit brown, some emphasis
of tone, as if I could starve
myself into a magnetic object,
bake myself into being, into
a female form that would draw him
back from journeys, from tracing
snowshoe paths across polar caps,
to a non-floating ground,
some warm earth we could inhabit.

The Magic Box

Handsome Mr. Fox eats up all his brides
before he's caught and "hacked into a thousand pieces"
in the old English story Peter used to tell.
In another, a fisherman is carried to shore
by a talking sea turtle who gives him a magic box,
tells him "don't look inside." But he does, as they all do
in stories. A thick cloud of purple smoke pours out
to age him instantly, to add all those years
he stayed young, while living with the queen of the deep
green undersea world. All his skin falls slack
and he dies.

          I think about Peter, his red-brown hair,
blue eyes, the blushing skin that covers the soft
grey cortex which won't leap now, lightning-fast,
through the synapses forming his stories. His brain
biopsy is scheduled for Tuesday, and Vita calls
me, the only one she knows who would know anything,
wants my opinion of the list of medicines that
she's copied down: sulfadiazine, acyclovir,
decadron, pentamadine, an anti-yeast. Then she asks
a mother's questions. "How many burr holes?"
"Is it too late for AZT?"

          The neurologist
told her the head scan looks like "cottage
cheese" and I know she means Swiss, as grey
lucencies grow black, expose the deficits
that his consciousness tries to cover by
confabulating: on the phone, he reports that
cats are chewing the bones of his toes at night,
that he's heard I travelled in the Soviet Union
for twelve years to look for medicines that work.
In this way he explains both my kindly interest
and my years of absence.

          When I moved out,
I took the Russian lacquer box that pictures a man,

red-bearded like Peter, kneeling as a golden
fish leaps from the blue swirling sea and opens
its mouth to speak. But he wouldn't let me keep
his bright painting of Caucasus women
with long braids, robed in traditional clothes,
flags flying behind them, or the book
with a woodcut of two children taking handfuls
from the gingerbread house, after they had eaten
all of Baba Yaga's fingers.

                He tells me the skin
on his backside is sunburned, raw, asks if
we put bars around people in California, jail them
in bed so they can't rise to urinate. I say yes,
he utters "How primitive," asks what to do
and I say "Go ahead," assuming the catheter
bag will catch it, echoing his story from
childhood in the thin-walled Dyckman Street project—
a neighbor child called to her mother at 3 a.m.
"Ma, I gotta pee" and the tired mother yelled back
"Go in the bed."

              I wonder if he remembers Mr. Fox's
motto, "Be bold, be bold, but not too bold,
lest your heart's blood run cold." I imagine
his wrists restrained with gauze, his thin torso
posied in the white geriatric vest, its long ties
anchoring him. It's designed for someone old, demented,
not Peter who's 38 when convolutions of brain
start to vanish, as they would have at 80. I remember
his skin, its fine-pored pinkness, almost translucent,
like a child's, then picture it now—lined
and opaque, fallen dough that won't rise.

Painting

He'd go down to the basement
wearing his dark blue work shirt,
to the corner of the windowless,
cinder-block room where he had
his canvas propped, and somehow,
after years of being tangled up
in knots of possibility, after
days of talk, after wrestling
with the angel of Not-painting,
he squeezed a wildly orange
Vermont landscape out of those
bright oily tubes, smeared it,
all its red-leafed, golden blur,
onto the rectangle of cloth
and gesso that had been waiting,
like me, for his stroking hand.

In the Morning

Like at the pool, trying to haul
        myself out, caught in that
                transition between air

and water, floundering for a moment
        on the concrete lip,
                at the alarm,

I surface awkwardly remembering I dreamt
        about Peter, I struggle
                to wake, and still

hold on to the slippery creature.
        In last night's phone call,
                a stranger answered

in the hospital room, said Peter was
        asleep so soundly
                he couldn't be roused.

I decide this is good, that he not
        be awake to feel
                the flicker of

himself begin to falter, as he starts
        to part company with
                the body. We used to

curl up together, like children, vying
        to be held and he'd always
                say—see you

in the morning, right before sinking off
        into the solitary pool
                of his first dream.

Communal Living

When we were young and immortal
what would we have said,
if an angel had come down
to our shack in Oregon's green
hills, as we warmed ourselves
beside the wood stove in a dark
soot-laden dawn, waiting for
Enid to make a pot of oatmeal,
for Wayne to chop more wood;

if she waded her way among the piles
of duffle bags, the psychedelic
watercolors, the cans of Bugler,
packs of Camels with rising suns,
waves of color and stars drawn on,
found us in overalls and hiking boots,
long cotton paisley skirts,
hair down past the waist, our manes
blowing in the smoky early morning
as we rolled our first cigarettes
or weed, maybe someone put on The Band,
Jackie Lomax or *Fresh Cream*.

She would furl her wings, point and
say—you, dead at 23, a suicide; you,
medical school; you, a life of loss and
unemployment; you, a mother, activist
in Vermont; you, filmmaker in Russia;
you, one year of law school, one son,
then dead at 40, an unnamed virus.
Would we have tilted back our
uncombed heads and laughed?

The Virus

Once, I thought there should be
a special circle of hell
for the infector, that
inoculating prick who drove
the virus deep inside your ass,
the butt thrusts asking for it,
an infinitesimal capsule of death
given in the lust spurt by some
anonymous quick fuck, or maybe
your long-time lover, your golden-
haired, "Over the Rainbow" tenor;
but then I remember, whoever he was,
he has this particular death
in store, watching his taut body
rot, his skin splotch, his mind go
and I think—who needs hell.

Blood Clot

This time it's his heart. He has
a tumor. In his heart. The size
of an egg. The meaty bag that pumps
him up, pinkens his skin, the bright eyes,
quickens the long painterly fingers,
this sack, his mother says, is full
of something that should not be there.
Her call pulls me back into the web,
after all these years. I think
how I'd nestle in his neck's hollow,
where they'll insert the needle and
catheter to fish for a chunk of tissue,
one small bite is all they need to tell
what form the wild cells take—myxoma,
lymphoma, Kaposi's sarcoma or something
so invasive it can eat a hole through
the wall in a matter of weeks. The cardiologist
gives odds, says no surgeon will touch him,
given the high mortality, not naming
the virus. So I go, cross country, eating
gelled bits of airline food. I travel to survey
the damage, to see what harm I've done.

                    At the Vermont station,
                    I stamped my feet to warm them,
                    to bring them partway back to life.
                    Behind the thick glass window,
                    Peter waved, impatient, looked
                    and waved again, ruddy-cheeked,
                    funeral-faced, called suddenly
                    to New York, after his Grandpapoose
                    was found dead on the floor,
                    a heart attack at 84, while
                    Grandmadam trembled in her long
                    black dress, the powdered mask
                    of her face, jailed behind her
                    aluminum walker, her parkinsonian

legs quivering, tiny in his big chair.
We spoke of getting old like them,
imagined our grandchildren coming
to visit us, white haired, full
of stories. We waited for the ponderous
train to puff up and depart, and
I felt a yank on the line between us;
then rage, when something I am as used to
as an old coat rips away.

At our venomous parting
when I told you—Drop dead—
that seed, my words,
planted in your heart
18 years ago, took
this long to bear fruit.
It took too long.

I was pleased to remember which bus
to take downtown, to disembark
from its lumbering hull at 23rd Street,
walk west jangling his borrowed keys
in the pocket of my California coat,
unlined for New York winter, an alien
on old familiar turf. Two locks.
Open the door. His place. Peter's dusty,
musty-aired place. Littered with trinkets
from his tour-guide days, endless
Russian lacquer dolls, Chinese cloisonné
vases, books from the store where we worked
on 57th Street, quirky, wood-floored, until
some chain bought and homogenized it.
Open the refrigerator, the milk frozen
solid in its carton, baloney, old Chinese
take-out moldering in greasy boxes.
Afraid to walk barefoot, I wear his slippers.
Later, in the shower, blue-green mold flowering
in the corners, copper green streaking the old

enamel tub, I think of fungi, bacteria, wonder
what lives here in his wake.

I want to see my power, to survey
the battlefield. Whose corpse
is this, I'll say, to his cool
white skin, collapsed like a slip
someone has just stepped out of.
Whose smell is this, I'll say,
each day as they open the shower-curtain
drape that circles the bed. He says
it's the only way he knows where he is,
when he wakes at night, he recalls
that home does not have this metal
track on the ceiling. They open
the curtain and each time, some
new field of flesh shows, chest
with the plastic EKG patches,
thighs, gown not pulled down,
urinal left propped there
and forgotten, the sagging generic
hospital gown, blue-printed cotton,
supposed to tie in the back, it hangs,
breakfast-flecked, loose at the neck.
And I see his neck, the puffed-up,
livid face swollen by steroids,
and those long narrow nostrils
I seem to be always looking up into
as I sit by the hospital bed, the oddness
of racing here to be bored, having
to think up things to say. On rounds
the doctors announce it's not a tumor today
but a clot, shifting in their scans
and echo fields, their sonar tracing
the aquatic chambers of his heart.

      I don't know how I knew it then, when
      I returned from the station, walked

back down the snow-plowed path to our dorm,
our room, curled onto the mattress
beside the pregnant cat, alone
for almost the first time in a young life,
that this was one of those fulcrums
where the balance shifts. Looking out
at the perilous four-foot-long icicles
hanging from the eaves above the poor
ignorant pedestrians plodding along
on the squeaky, snow-packed path, I knew—
sooner or later, something would fall.

It's an art—
the word spoken,
the curse embedded,
the robe poisoned,
a toxin dropped
in the ear.

They said that whatever is wrong with
his spine weakens his doughy legs,
predisposes him to clots. One nested
in his heart, broke, showered his lungs
with emboli, so now he gasps for air
whenever he speaks from behind that green,
see-through plastic mask, a plicated hose
anchoring him to the oxygen.
His three year old son said—
Papa, you look like an elephant.
Here at St. Vincent's they put a crucifix
in every room. It's where, someone said,
Dylan Thomas died his sloppy death.
The air is thick with charity.

I wondered if we'd die in the dark,
as I felt nostrils ice, lungs sting,
saw frost form on his red beard

and held his long mittened hand,
so padded I could feel
no hand, only down. I hated
the squeak of packed snow under crepe
soles. Other couples, all disturbed
in one way or another, would visit
and he'd blanket us under layers
of sound, play music or lecture us
on Lake Baikal, the Polaris expedition,
Indian religions, bride prices,
the sati story—how the loyal,
living wife burns on her husband's pyre.
I'd crochet black-bordered squares
for the afghan that grew large enough
to cover our contiguous twin beds.
I timed each square at twenty minutes,
measured out my brightness this way,
poured it into our shroud.

The bathroom faucet won't turn off,
the humid air must breed algae, mildew.
What could I catch, standing naked
in his tub, what could enter when
I brush my teeth, melt milk for coffee,
lie on his uncomfortable blue sheets?
Is this his pillow where I press
my sleeping face? In the morning
I pack one book from his shelves,
one with my name in it, Chinese poems.
His keys in my pocket, I walk south,
turn on Twelfth Street, past
the brownstone where we rented
one room, slept in a single bed. I'd sit
holding the painted Spanish cup, look out
the window at the hospital, watch
nurses come and go. Now I enter to give
the warm keys into his still-warm hands.

I remember my crib's flannel blanket,
mantle of comfort, torn from my shoulders
years later, like skin. Peter clings
to the body like this, does not give up
as it unravels, does not reject his legs
when they stop working, his numb hands
when they begin to drop things and he has
to ask to be fed, his mind, when he finds large
pockets of memory gone. He turns to the wall,
wanders in thick webs of tangential thought,
and swaddled in the tattered flesh, holds on.

I'll watch you die
your one death. It should
have been one of your plays,
well-rehearsed, words measured,
not our impromptu efforts
at goodbye, not your scream,
"Don't you see what this means?
I'm going to die."

I picture his egg-size clot,
its glossy surface partly clogging
the heart's valves, bits break off,
flow downstream, meaty messengers,
permeate the pink airiness of his lungs,
lodge there, coagulate further islands
of lung, clotting dark venous blood—
a fat black hen rustles noisy feathers,
settling into its last red nest.

When he suddenly announced his leaving
I wondered how I'd caused the transformation
and thought—was it my mouth, some rotten
meat scent exhaled across the pillow?
Or the cunt, its fleshy layers
issuing some clouded fluid, foreign
to his touch, his tongue. Did my largeness

make for fears I'd swallow him, break
the white crust of his bones, like
eating quail, that thin, brittle crack?
Was it my blood, did the sheet blots
frighten him, remind him of where
he'd come from, of loss, of threat?
What had him look at me, and say
he'd never, never sink into such
a well again? Was it terror?
He must have fled for his life.

Nothing in. Nothing
out. The silence
is perfect, except
for that insistent
meat-red motor that
somehow keeps the fluid
circling through its
veiny circuits. Each
drop from the transparent
bags, plastic udders
hung from metal hooks,
enters his saline
blood. Peter loved
red meat with salt.
It's all that's left
of him. That and
the sea-glass blue
of his half-closed eyes.

You can't go simply.
not without the old curse
blooming. It's what you get,
you fool. It was your choice.
Leaving was your choice.
And this is mine. I did not
invent the microorganisms.
I could not dream up CMV, PCP,

toxoplasmosis of your soft
grey brain, the ungodly virus
itself, chewing away, with
icy teeth, at your spinal cord.
They are my instruments.
I wished your death and
here they are. It doesn't
teach the lesson that I'd
hoped for. It's the same old
fucking loss. The glacier that
freezes us in place for centuries,
the same old separateness, only
this time it's called death.
How dare you do it to me
one more time.

I think of his brain, softening,
a half-cooked yolk bumping
against its enamel shell,
the shell about to crack,
to release him
out of his nested home.
It's the will of the body—
it wants to rot,
a basic yearning to return
to earth, to rupture the bonds
of constraining cells
and break free.

I came to throw the first
spade of dirt. Sorry
it gets in your eyes.
I thought you'd be dead
by now. It should have been
that first fall, you watching
the Vermont foliage turn
orange, me watching Riverside
Park go cold and dark, when

I had to listen closely
to tell if my own kicked
heart still thumped.
It took too long for the net
I cast to thicken your blood.

He's asleep when I come back from shopping—
a Van Gogh corn field for the wall, not
the one with crows, Christmas presents,
Puss in Boots and an *Alice* for the son
who is his, not the one we imagined.
I sit in a stiff-backed chair under
the crucifix, his black umbrella dripping
puddles on hospital linoleum, as he breathes
a little while longer through those narrow
nostrils, the reddish hair now going grey,
the pink skin, ashen, translucent lids hiding
the wintery blue dimming of his eyes.

Slides

They'll double-glove
to slice his brain.
Some neurologist will be
overjoyed to own the slides.
"Like scattershot to
the cortex" they said,
"the remarkable clinical
picture…euphoric
paranoia…islands
of memory preserved."

They'll show the slides
at Mortality Conference,
the differential diagnosis
of viral dementia,
toxoplasmosis, his
convoluted brain up there
in front of everyone
in eosin or silver stain,
neurons crackling across
the reflective screen.

He loved those subway
photographs, four shots
for 75 cents. He'd plan
the poses, raise an
eyebrow, show his teeth.
"For history" he said,
so his grandchildren
could admire his ponytail,
his new leather coat.
He loved a display.

Carriage

In Moscow, the day after you died,
some desiccated Generals declared
they'd run the show. The next day,
a hundred thousand people at the
Winter Palace said they wouldn't.

You'd mailed me postcards from
the Kremlin, from Samarkand, Tashkent,
a photograph of the first tsar's
fur-rimmed crown. We'd named a kitten
Azerbaijan, just for the joy of those
purred syllables in the throat.

Your Grandmadam, a country girl,
said she was thrilled to see Gorky
on Nevsky Prospekt. She emptied
diapers out her St. Petersburg window,
brought the baby to a meeting,
his crying bothered everyone, his
squawking grew louder, then Lenin
told her "Ria, take the baby home."

You loved that scene in *Potemkin*,
the carriage rocking down steps,
a flight of its own, a motherless,
driverless baby tumbling down
through history. Was it like that,
to leave your body, to fall away
who knows where, to leave a white carcass
on the unwatched tundra of those sheets?

Thief

I never know how the dead will wake me,
a sudden glimpse of the cobalt blue
of your corduroy shirt, or turning a page,
I'm startled by Dürer's *Self-portrait
in Coat with Fur Collar* and think
I've found your lost photograph.

I dreamt someone was stealing your books,
the da Vinci, the Abrams Gauguin,
the whole architecture section,
Hokusai prints. We came home and found
shelves emptied, dropped volumes with
injured spines. I told the detective—
Peter will die soon—and showed him
where we hid the unopened books,
inside the back of the grandfather clock.
I woke to examine my criminal hands.

I thought you were light, your witch-red
halo of hair, metallic blue eyes,
Blake's Lucifer burning, or Anterrabae,
the Falling God. Turning in air, shedding
embers, rays illuminate the dark tunnel
through which, Alice-like, you fall.

A hyena, I don't wait to chew your bones.
You have blessed me with your impermanence,
this faint thumbprint pressed on my forehead,
left liquid to evaporate, or the cup's silver rim,
cold at my lips. Now we're married to paper.
I have taken you in. I am fed. Am I then the thief?

Ashes

Vita and I consider his
hatred of ceremony. Her
last visit, in the morgue,
she rubbed his inert arm,
the familiar flesh with no

feeling left inside it,
tallow-colored, transformed
into a thing: Peter, who hated
change, except for his romance
with the idea of revolution.

In our words, we've worked
the metamorphosis already,
his combustion into
other elements, the simple
unblessedness of the organic.

We envision the brothers,
summoned from Savannah, Moscow,
Brooklyn, chanting something
on the Staten Island Ferry,
as we dump ashes into the bay.

I imagine a grey swirl of grit
as mineral anoints the living,
as he's blown down into our
uttering throats, our hollow lungs,
into our transparent eyes.

TWO

The Lie

My mother is a coffin,
I shall not wake.

The body is warm meat
sealed off from language.
Each place, each part

unspoken, they died
in the dark, not called
to life by their names.

I seem a grown woman,
separate: this is a lie.

I am still inside
her pelvic bowl, bound
by the spiral-muscled

sack that grew to fit
my form, so elastic
it never said—Go.

Not being born, I can't
die. I refuse to be alone.

There is only one
of us. Loss does not
exist in our vocabulary.

The Knot

HOME

As a child you asked—how did I ever get into that
        spidery place, how could I ever get out.

Knowing more about food than sex, the child answered—
        she ate me in the broken shapes of meat

chunks, bone sticks, blood mush, then cast me out
        through that disturbing door

to the universe. It grew no clearer, even after
        searching your own pink folds.

You keep the child's dream—that if you do something
        right, just be tall enough, strong

enough, wise enough, you can fill the grown woman
        three times your size. The joy—to enter

again the warm clear pool where each move is met
        by resilient muscle as you float

upside down along glossed surfaces in that one safe
        place in the galaxy, the first

home, where you could exist inside your skin and
        not be alone. So you strive

for this heart of the world and just as you think
        you'd be able, then comes the fear—

if you penetrate this black gullet, the center,
        you'll dissolve. Swallowed up

in the thick mire of her tubes and guts, you will
        be, not near her, or like her, but her.

THE KNOT

The complex knot of the heart grew from
            those two cells

buried in a deep-sunken chamber of her
            body. Furrowed

wet layers dilate to surround the gilled
            creature who breathes

through her blood, swims in the amnion's
            salt sea, bound

to her by rope-like veins, uses her
            to ingest the world,

to take bread and air and sun,
            to metabolize

and bring them in, the rich liquid
            food of dreams.

       •

Change comes when the knobbed curl grows
            skin. The vulnerable

knot of the heart takes up its own beat
            not keeping time

with hers, but a counterpoint—the first
            separation;

the safeness of one new wall in between,
            the terror—it won't

hold and you'll be one more morsel of meat
            inside her, digested

into her vast shape as your fragile form
  vanishes, as water

is sucked from your small cells to feed the huge
  ocean of her.

THE TRAP

It's death in here, folded in
            on yourself so closely,

limb creases become permanent.
            Deprived of sight,

no motion of air in or out of
            the chest's fragile cage,

a stalk intrudes through your open
            belly, to carry vessels

and yolk. You hear blood percolate
            in the boggy filter

beside you, an umbrella shelters you
            from her serous fluids.

            •

Now membranes bind tighter and
            the walls glow red,

as when a child stares at the sun
            through cupped hands. If you

can only find the source of light,
            go there, before contractions

squeeze all your insides out. You can't
            stretch anymore and even

the Buddha would tire of this posture,
            knees bent, each muscle

prepared to extend and release,
            if she'll just let go.

THE FEAST

What kept you safe in that muscle-bound, pear-shaped
        nursery, where you simmered, one large

delicacy, arranged in rosette folds, more precise and
        improbable than those carved radishes and

Chinese carrots cut by pinking shears? What protected you
        from the caustic enzymes of her spit, her sharp bile,

the water-sucking loops of her bowel? The frail wall
        between you, a cellular veil in the placenta's

segments, where coils of your vessels baste in pockets
        of her blood, could collapse at any moment,

like the highway's concrete slabs crush cars and bodies flat
        amid sirens, burnt plastic and metal smells,

where, if you call in the dark, after the sky and
        ground have merged, no one will come.

How can you escape the sticky mesh of her grasp when
        the imprecise curls of your fingers can't push her

away as she enters your thorax, surrounds the red lobes
        of your small struggling heart? Her black milk

curdles your stomach. Her acid breath clouds your corneas,
        so no light can break through as she blankets you.

Bound here, you can't break out, there are no doors
        but those she controls and her only desire

is to swallow and swallow, for the joy, the fullness,
        as her rounded prow cuts a swath through the world.

OUT OF THE GARDEN

You lie nestled beside the blue-veined sponge
        that hums all day.

In the placenta's cotyledon-lined bowl, small
        spiny trees spread their villous

branches to feed you. In this loamy bed
        everything sprouts floridly,

a giant peony blooms from its spiral stalk.
        Or, you hide in this humid place

under the mushroom dome while peculiar fungal
        foldings emerge from your rounded skull,

pale cartilage curls of ear lobes, nostrils,
        the gap of pink lips.

       ·

Alert to each quake of the arable plot
        where you've grown, you wake in terror

when the ground gives way. Water drains
        leaving you beached, to bump

against sides without buoyancy. Contact
        of muscle on new red skin

burns now with friction when the walls
        start to press, as if with a will

to force you somewhere, to pluck your twiney
        unbranched stem. A deluge rips

loose the vascular roots, you're expelled.
        And now time begins.

THE POEM

Did I enter like this, head first, emerge
        from her blood-soaked crotch, that fork

at the base of the world? Was she conscious then
        when my head, after pounding for hours

at the door, broke through the membranes,
        ripped open the seal to pour forth

as my bony forehead tore her to make way
        for the wide diameter of shoulders,

the easy glide of torso, the spurt of pink legs
        with their afterthought, toe buds,

in that one moment we're allowed at her core?
        Did I search for air as I lost

my borrowed breathing, in the gasp that
        closes the last patent window

of my loculated heart, rechannels blood
        away from her vessels so it travels

only the small sea bound by my skin,
        sealing the distance between us?

The inrush of cold opens the arbor of lungs
        to emerge in a cry. Were they

her fluids or mine that clogged the pores
        of the nose, the base of the throat,

that gorge, where a raw sound rose out of me,
        born into the mortal world?

THE SIGN

The closed O at the belly's
center, site
of arterial bond to the large

one who holds us inside all those
months, while we
turn and kick without thought

of her, our room, bound by a rubbery
tube from this
twisted whorl to the place we feed—

the placenta, tangle of veins, thick
meaty crescent,
by which we know her, our common

membrane, whose one dark root
breaks, leaves
us scarred for life, her sign

printed in flesh in our middle,
omphalos,
embodies the pull that draws

our dark blood back down the spiral,
anchors us,
through a deciduous surface,

to her.

Persephone

I

Under the tiresome flat brightness
of sun, everything sticks in the humid air,
especially flesh. Her opaque powdered skin,
surrounding arms and presented cheek
sicken me. Can't she see I've grown
beyond a mother's embrace. The endless
candy tints of flowers, clothes, boats
and fruit all cloy. It takes years
for shallow August to melt into September.
I hate the smell of her orchards, overripe
apples rot on the grass, covered
by swarms of bees whose abdomens pump
in delight. I live for the first cold
twilight, the dry leaf scent, the color
of dark gold everywhere, deepening,
when the long, purple shadows signal
my coming escape, when the sun's
more oblique angle will bring him,
his black eyes, the depth of night.

II

I won't go. Or, when he who drains
all color from the earth comes
to claim me, I'll show him what ice is.
I'll be numb as death to his touch,
shrouded inside like a bulb's dormant core.
I hate her for making a bargain
that links my fate to the sun's decline.
Can't it stay September, when the fields
swarm with grain, bowing the tired stalks,
when bright melons grow round to the point
of bursting and everything is ripe,
fecund, and the apple, in its red heaviness
cleaves to the bough? Can't we stay
at this moment of fullness, all formed,
ready for birth, but not going, so
our closeness does not end with the first

cold night, when the dark other,
who plucks all fruit, arrives
to take me into that separate world?

III

There is no place without loss
as I shunt between two worlds,
timed to that huge burning star.
When day enlarges to outlast night,
I'm banished from his presence,
rise above ground. Either he is gone,
my large dark partner, and although
I dread his gaze, or think I may not
survive the pairings, I still feel
the icy pull, the deadly penetration
of desire; or I am missing her,
the mother whose brightness feeds me
honey, grains, apricots, in the long
summer grass under a lavish sun. I could
drown in her beauty, remain an infant
forever, or dissolve in her arms,
if there were no necessity of leaving,
no longing for return, regular
as equinox, to his deep world.

Balance Point

Imagine lifting the ball
of the foot, the socket
joint, balance point,
small fulcrum of the body,
placing it down expecting
firm earth and finding
nothing, no contact, no
matter pushing back from
the globe's coverings,
it would be like that,
a world without her;
imagine the particular
constellation, the state
of affairs where
a father disappoints,
flounders in his task
of cleaving the pair—
flat fish, two-eyes-up—
collapses into scaled
muscle and smell and
sticky fins gluing
to his shiny dead sides;
or where a mother, young,
unsure, can't release
the drooling child who
hovers at her knees,
the mother is not content
to fade, needs to be
not another planet circling
through the sky, but the bald
sun itself, morning's face
seared in memory for life,
so her risings and settings
clock everyone's days
like an old testament
figure warning in a rumbling
voice that is always just
behind your shoulder, whose

piercing eye always watches
from the sky—*the Lord thy*
God is a jealous God, and
she can't survive without
you, looking up, admiring;
how could you wound her,
choose to grow up, sprout
breasts, litter the field
with your cyclical blood
on ground already taken,
none remains unclaimed,
no meadow of wheat and poppies
waits for your faint-haired
feet to plant themselves,
no place to find there
in the mirror, her daughter,
brown-eyed, long-jawed
balancing her awkward skull
on top of a rigid spine
which sends its rib-branches
forward in white half-circles
that duplicate a mother's arms
or interlaced fingers, caging
there, that meaty embryo, your
heart, which she wants for
dinner each day and each day
you humbly, eagerly give it
saying—*take this, my flesh*,
swallow me, keep me inside,
safe, my heavenly jailer,
I ask you to throw away
the key, I'll renounce
the world, am willing
to stay with no regret,
no wish to stretch outdoors,
stand upright among equals,
I prefer your company
to mortals, give thanks

for each morsel you send me,
the rich and plentiful air
piped in, the peace of being
well housed, a room designed,
appointed perfectly for me:
your savior, sparing you
from the knife of my *No*,
saying I can't live here
forever, you are not
my earth and firmament,
it is me who will consume
and digest you, keeping
what nourishment I need,
tossing the bones aside
on the ancestral heap,
it is not fatal, our dance
of embrace and separation,
you won't really die, if
I place my foot down and
it finds, not the horizon
of your breast, not your
breath firing and filling,
expiring your life out
into my mimicking soul,
but solid ground.

THREE

The Biopsy

The dapper surgeon enters, greets me
loudly, hangs his coat on a steel hook
next to my slip, as in a cozy household.
I lie down and we begin. He preps
with those large orange Q-tips—
betadine swabs—poking objectively,
then asks for lidocaine and fussily
tells the nurse to wipe the top
of the unopened bottle with alcohol.

The fine needle stings, bites deeper.
He arranges the green cloth drapes,
the last has an open square at its center,
so my now-orange nipple protrudes through,
one spot of nakedness among our hospital gowns,
an absurd striptease. Now the silver
dish-lights are focused on this point,
the small flesh star, from which
the whole scene radiates. He calls
for a #15 blade, which then glides
without pain, just a pull.

I had thought my skin was a permanent seal.
Now I watch this layer of myself,
this pale field, sprout red flowers
in a sudden watercoloring,
as the scalpel makes its first nick,
then the dark trail blooms, spills over.

A wet trickle crosses my ribs,
and he asks for the cautery.
It crackles, clotting off small vessels,
making a tasty smell of fat,
like chicken skin frying. He sets
the handle down on the drape
half across my face. Caught
in the rhythm of his concentrated
breathing, I close my eyes, hear

the metallic nips of his scissors,
feel the quick daubs of gauze.
Trying to be elsewhere,
I think of the morning paper,
but only remember the photographs—
the planetary curve of Neptune,
the shadow of its Great Dark Spot.

When he calls for the chromic, I know
I'm now being repaired. I glance down
to find my nipple being lifted
off to the right, grasped by
the stainless-steel teeth of the forceps,
beside a meaty red hole, empty now,
its small harvest reaped. I picture
the journey of the dense, yellow marble
with blood-tinged edges, this aborted
piece of me, travelling to the lab
in a clear bottle of formalin,
where they'll set it in wax,
layer it by microtome, then examine
each section, my cellular patterns.

Suturing the red place, he asks
how I'm doing, his first words.
I gaze at him, his all-white hair,
his smile as he says that the nodule
will prove benign, this man
who went beyond my skin
as no one else has, to see my body
opened by his working hands,
as he made me for the first time, his.

Anorexia

Not everyone is so skilled
at the ancient art, not everyone
can exist on air, refusing
the burden of flesh. Hating

the yellow globs of fat in any
form—under the skin, padding
the heart, cushions for the eyes'
globes, but mostly those

that mark her as her mother's—
the encumbering curves of hip
or breast, she eats only
oranges and water, a cannibal

of self. Trying to undo all
the knots the female body has
tied, the cyclical obligations
to gush, to feed, she chooses

to hone her shape down,
her scapulae prepared like
thin birds, to fly away from
the spine. Barely held together

by silk and liquid and air,
she floats, flightless, the water's
iciness along her back;
she tries not to be sucked

down by the black cold,
its deadliness pulling
at the nape of her long neck,
biting at her unfeathered heels.

The Pool

At the University, we are just visitors,
borrowing lanes while our pool is repainted,
dislocated older swimmers dropped into the deep end,
ill-fitted to this slick and technical place

that the college racers call a fast pool.
Less sleek than the team, more lumpy and lined
than the water polo players, we are unused
to spotlights, the too bright portholes

of light that intrude on this turquoise
underwater world. We were used to eucalyptus
leaves floating in our algaed, peeling tank,
to evening swallows dipping their beaks, swooping

down to drink. Once in twilight, dark enough
to watch moonrise during the backstroke laps,
a deer walked by the ivy-laden wall. But here,
foreigners, washing in communal showers

in a large, well-lit room of chrome and tile,
we see each has her wound—the woman with one
breast, two with horizontal belly scars, fat
sagging above the lines, one just returned,

her sternum marked by a new red incision,
so we know her chest was split like a chicken
breast and we wonder what was taken.
As we stand there on thousands of tiny

blue squares, under jets of hot water, rinse
the caustic chlorine out of our hair,
each one thinks about wholeness and wants
to go home to our mossy mother pool.

Undertow

The furniture returns from the
upholsterer dressed in fabric identical
to that in my mother's living room,
I am turning into her, I say, as I

look into the whitening room, *I am
her echo*, I say to the mirror, seeing
the pad under my eyebrow become heavy,
with time, and sag, the shape of the eye

now matching hers, only the quality
of brown remains mine; there's that
visceral tug, like a pulse, so constant
it goes unheard, blood's undertow;

and at this moment the overlooked cat
brings an orange-throated bird into the
kitchen, its neck flops, but chirps still
pepper the air, scatter like the downy

underfeathers, so difficult to clean up,
flying away from the wind of the broom,
that I've learned to use damp paper
towels to catch the feathers and

the birdblood, so different from ours
that it's recognized under the microscope
with ease; the few stray drops, their
splatter prints strewn across the linoleum,

lead in a bright red trail to the site
she's chosen for the final dismembering,
proudly licking her lips, almost says
mother, look at me, my quickening gift.

The Cadaver

I

Overwhelmed by smell, warned
by this ancient sense, you approach
the body, cool and supine
on the chrome table. This rubbery
thing will show you the mysteries
as you open his insides,
expose them to fluorescent light
and the lab's cold air. Sick
of looking, hating the slippery
touch that pickles your finger tips
into ridges, as if you'd been in the tub
all day, you fly out through the double
doors to pace the hard linoleum,
breathe air free of formaldehyde,
feel your separateness in the swing
of your legs, your bladder fullness,
and blood-pumped warmth. You list
your differences from the inert man
who teaches you the body's form and names,
who teaches you the body's death.

II

On your schedule, it says Gross Anatomy Lab
so you're all on time, cluster
around the doorway to be outside
of the odor and at some distance
from the silent shapes on the tables.
A white-coated instructor appears,
with the look of a dapper marine,
calls out names from his list by fours.
You're bunched with three other J's,
white males, who check out each others'
equipment—the blue plastic boxes
of scalpels and probes, the atlas
in paper or hardback, opaque latex gloves.
They notice your metzenbaum scissors

stolen from a summertime lab job.
While the text begins with the chest
and you read in advance, he says start
with the forearms and places two of you
on each side of the damp sheet
that covers something. While you wait
for your first look at death, the level
of laughter rises, as among soldiers
nearing the enemy front.
Later, you walked to the car,
a collection of fragments,
disarticulated bones, muscle spindles,
vessels and nerves, you wondered
what held you together. At home
the cats wouldn't come near you
even after a shower. And you thought
you'd never be a whole animal again.

III

Older than your father,
with trim beard, wry facial lines
and dilated pupils, you imagine the name
Joseph for him, not thinking then
of the father who had so little to do
in the old story, who after the annunciation
only sheltered the divine parasite,
like a bewildered bird
constantly feeding the fat cuckoo
placed in his small nest.
In this way the cadaver fathered
knowledge, provided no live seed,
but gave the place for learning,
its food and shelter. You explored
the deep nest of the thorax, held
by the springy bows of the ribs,
the deep gutters linked
to the paraspinal troughs, that emptied

into the dark hole of the pelvis.
You knew these hollows like home,
almost comfortable there
once you'd cleaned out the matted meat
of the right upper lobe
that was once aerated lung,
before the cancer ate it.
You wondered who this was,
who would make the sacrifice
and freely give that which
used to be stolen from graves.
Didn't they imagine their bodies
picked over by cannibals, hungry
for learning, who would expose
their insides, take parts away
in avid hands, to consume
each shred of flesh?
Didn't they know there'd be jokes—
the young husband leaving his
cadaver-mate wife a Valentine's note
tucked inside the left ventricle?
Who would choose this way
to stretch their time above ground?
Would they have thought only
of the slow gestation, embedded
in some student's cortex, to form
a lifetime's template for all
future bodies—patients and lovers?

IV
There weren't enough corpses
to go around, so several students
shared, each played out some
internal drama on the body
of the dead father, and like unruly
children growing self-assured, quarreled
often. You fought over who would expose
the optic nerve, who severed the trochlear.

One morning you arrived
to find that the obsessive lab partner
had wrestled the cadaver
into lithotomy position to dissect
the pelvic floor, had started at 6 a.m.
and finished before you arrived.
So you probed and learned the places,
all the cutting being done.
In the territorial battles over forearms
and hearts, the things with many segments
to learn, or intricate nerve ramifications
and muscle insertions, for these
there was an aluminum bin of parts.
You could sit on high wooden stools
around the table and examine spare limbs,
pull each tendon, watch which finger rose,
make disembodied fuck-you signs
at each other's backs.

V

The instructor shows a tape
of highlights, before doing
the pelvis. The actor playing
doctor says "First eviscerate
the abdomen" and you clench
your teeth as they show
someone scooping out the guts.
Then, "The best approach
to the pelvic viscera
is the sagittal section."
And they show someone
pretend to cut (it had been done
in advance) down the midline
and lift away the whole leg
and groin and half the pelvis,
separate it from the body
en bloc, then zoom
to the remaining half a uterus,

one ovary and fallopian tube.
It was that silent lifting away
one quarter of the body
leaving clean-cut edges,
that, more than any battle film,
had the cool and precise quality
of a recurrent nightmare's inevitable end.

VI
A dream full of walking corpses
came in the second week. You grew
uncertain in the days, worried
about your skin and thought
what a huge burden to hold in
all that is in there—
the glistening viscera packed
under a ciear omentum. You remember
in grade school the day
they showed an anatomical picture,
it was the moment you realized
that the tube that led
from your mouth did not open up
on an empty black vault,
but that the insides were full
of colors and bulges, large
purple shapes, and were pleased
to find yourself so rich
and well housed; but scared
that the thinness of walls
would burst from the pulsing
pressure of all those organs,
those nameless things—all that
just to take peas and carrots
and bread and grind it up
into shit. You knew then
there were things that no one
had told you, grew alarmed
to find your safe shelter

part of the secret. And this
terror surfaced in nightmares—
the basement full of dead bodies
that sit up when you enter, roll
their eyes, stand on detachable legs,
wave their own and others' hands
as they perform some tribal dance
that you are part of.
You watch as one lies down, uses
the saw to split her own thorax,
opens her heart to the air.

VII

Field guides taught those who learned
each coastal shrub and bird,
who needed to know the word
for each tree to hold off darkness
in the woods. Or, it was their way
to love the world, to recite
the names for things that grow,
our sibling creatures. We each
tame wilderness by naming it.
You wanted to find your way
in the world of flesh, surprised
to find yourself embodied so,
born out of the unyielding place
where you swam, a small fish
sealed in shiny membranes, bound
within muscular layers, suspended
by the round ligaments, until expelled,
a piece of earth's strange biology.
You remember as a child finding places
which no one would say aloud,
their functions or their pleasures.
These things with weight and texture
could be felt by your palpating fingers,
their details encompassed by the eye.
You believe the knowledge

and its recitation can almost
hold off death. When your tongue pronounces:
intertrochanteric fossa, greater and
lesser omentum, orbicularis oculi, ·
splanchnic bed, pubic symphysis,
hallucis longus, ciliate ganglion,
you think this lore will keep
the body warm and whole,
so sensation won't dissolve the walls.
Like a child says prayers in the dark
in a language she doesn't know,
or an infant in the crib rubs
her mouth, tastes her fingers,
for the soothing friction of flesh,
and to know that hand and lips are there,
or thrashes to know what arms contain her,
you name the parts to know the edges hold,
will keep inside the disparate forces
that push in their own directions,
threaten to burst the boundaries,
flood the surface, annihilate you.

    VIII
As you worked on the thigh, bisected
the long strap of the sartorius, admired
the pinnate shape of the rectus femoris,
separated the pectineus, adductor longus,
gracilis, followed the great saphenous vein
into the pocket of the femoral canal
in its row of nerve, artery, vein and ligament,
someone walked in carrying a radio,
and you heard them announce the fall
of Saigon, the end of the war, and then
went back to removing pads of dense
yellow fat to carve out muscles,
trace them from origin to insertion,
so they look like sculpture
more than the dissection of death.

54

You return to your small quiet war
where you're willing to pay the blood price
to master the body, its frailties,
to prove yourself armored, able,
untouched by scenes of carnage.
They were like the images left
from the summer's job, where you prepped
dogs for the heart surgeons to practice
transplant techniques. That meant
walk to the 17th floor to fetch
a lab dog, wild and unused to humans,
lead it down to the concrete-floored room,
bind its muzzle with a slipknot,
shave the forepaw, inject the nembutal IV,
quickly intubate, then tie the heavy thing,
spread-eagled, to the metal table,
do cut downs for arterial lines
in the soft folds of the groin,
then with the cautery, open the skin,
a smell of burnt fur and fried fat,
then take the bone saw to crack the sternum,
wedge it apart with the retractors'
metal jaws, cover the rib ends with paraffin
to keep the field dry, slice open
the pericardium, tie it like a sling,
cradling the still beating red heart,
wired now to monitors, then mop up the blood,
stand aside to play scrub nurse
and watch the real surgeons begin.

IX
Gauze towels swathe the head,
resembling some bedouin's
or mummy's, and all of you
choose to keep the covers on
after that one first look
at this most human of parts
with its soft bony planes,

places you know have been stroked,
kissed, the flare of nostrils,
the frail curve of eyelid,
the glimpse of pink tongue.
Your group stands and looks, uncertain
in their own bodies, so you volunteer
and make the tentative first cuts
across the scalp, then finding it tough
and thick as grapefruit rind,
cut more deeply, down to the fibrous layers.
You quarter it, slide the blade's
handle end in to separate the fascia
attachments, making a velcro-like sound.
You bare the rounded bones, peel
the edges of scalp down past the eyebrows,
with relief, you cover the eyes,
and wait for the diener to come
with his bone saw, which in its noisy
harmlessness stops at flesh
and only cuts denser stuff.
You watch him prop the head
to saw the horizontal circle,
making a smell of burned bone,
then take his chisel, whack it
for the final pop, like the sound
of a coconut cracked open,
and on this last hinge, lift
the shallow ivory bowl to expose
the familiar convolutions
of grey matter that your brain
will begin to examine.

     X
Valhalla of cadavers, where
hospital-slain heroes will themselves
into your inexperienced hands, here
you learn the labels for all

the structures of your mute
first patient. He didn't quicken
under your omnipotent touch.
He did not wake, speak or
rise from the dead. Instead,
his useful death fed you. His meat,
preserved above ground, formed a feast,
served on a silver table. Just as
your father filled you with knowledge,
to make you like him, not her,
the body's names formed a knife edge
that cleaved you two. He lifted
you out of her confining lap,
out of the glacier where you and she
were frozen, where the skin surfaces
stuck like a tongue to iced metal.
He ripped you loose, left you still feeling
the red rawness of your attachment.
Then he gave you words to seal the surface,
to heal you, make you whole.
At night you feel disloyal
as you nestle your bony head
on the bowed twigs of someone's ribs,
listen to the regular clicks
as his heart's valvular leaflets
open and close. You consider
the cusps' clock-like rhythm,
remember their texture, these
small invisible pocketed flaps.
You start naming the shapes
that lie under your hand, within
this mortal body you've clung to
after leaving the others, after
moving away from the too small
nest of the father's chest, of
the mother's arms, having
with knives, delivered yourself.

XI

So how do they dispose of the bodies,
you asked, rinsing scraps off your hands,
down the drain of the stainless steel sink,
where you'd washed the sludge out
of the large bowel so you could examine
haustral markings and the cecal valve.
They said all the parts
are saved for burial or cremation
and you wondered how they know
who's who, if all these people
commingle in death, fill
each other's graves. You imagine
the burning bodies looking
like those from the dog lab
after you dumped them into
the hospital's main incinerator—
the sudden brushfire of fur
and skin, the flames folding
into the dark evacuated cavities
to be extinguished there
or at high heat eat through
the smooth-surfaced walls,
leaving ignited patches of bone.
You want to utter some blessing
when you pull up the sheet the last time,
over his familiar body. You wonder
if you'll think of him, your model
of death, when you fold mottled hands
across your chest as it ceases to rise
and fall, as you exhale from the bottom
of your lungs and the air grows still
in the small caverns of your nostrils,
as heartbeats dissolve into fibrillation,
muscle fibers lock, all sphincters
give way and you drop to room temperature,
your dilated eyes gazing at nothing.

XII

Having fed like a worm on the bones of the dead
or like a bird, on the body's worms,
you grow large and leave home
prepared for your adult life
of minding the sick, performing
technical procedures on the dying.
You know where you are
when, after your young patient dies,
you go to the morgue, see them place
her on the elevated metal table,
hear the dozens of aluminum-tipped ends
of her cornrowed braids clatter
as they fall away limply
from her blue-lipped face. You watch
her resilient skin give way
under the bright blade as they open
the large flaps of her body's walls,
sever the great vessels, lift out
her heart and lungs in one piece,
hung from the cartilage handle
of her trachea. You recite the branches
as they trace her pulmonary arteries
searching for the clot that killed her.
On the hospital wards, there are moments
that remind you of the lab, when you tell
the old man to turn his head, so you can
insert the needle in his jugular, enter beside
the belly of the sternocleidomastoid.
You know how it wraps its tendon
along the clavicle, feel the vein's
sheath give, watch the paper drape
over his breathing face lift for a second,
then you forget again that this meat
you dig in is warm and pulsing,
as you aim your precise hand
at the visible landmarks of the unseen world
whose map now lies in your mind.

Brother and Sister

Flying back around the world to L.A.,
a smoggy return, he thought about
ceramic jars of corn placed inside
tombs. Osiris made it sprout, food
for the journey, and a promise
of resurrection made by the lord
of the Otherworld, who had known death
himself, had fathered a child with his twin
sister-spouse as she hid in the reeds,
holding his laid-out corpse.

                They began
the morphine drip at home, hoping to cloud
her consciousness, hoping she would begin
a comfortable sail down this last river,
but she woke up and they invited all
the relatives back for one more visit.
Tired, she couldn't hold her eyes open,
asked them to leave, then said, after
60 years together, she wouldn't leave earth
without embracing her brother.

                He'd seen
the papyrus showing the dead one led
by jackal-headed Anubis to the judgment hall.
The deceased's heart is weighed against
the feather of truth, and if the scale tips,
he's instantly consumed by the sharp-toothed
Eater of the Dead. If the balance holds,
the man is introduced to Osiris and to Isis,
who had found and assembled all of her husband's
scattered, severed parts.

                He scanned her
with his surgeon's eye, the swollen belly,
the bloated lids, the withered skin,
fetor, and thought—it will be tonight.
But in the morning she sat up wanting sips

of water, amazing everyone, her body's
tenacity, the skillful cells, at her age,
adapting to work in new surroundings,
in their efforts, cleansing her uremic
blood, keeping her breathing.

                  He'd said
she was a goner 15 years before, when
the newfound cancer was everywhere and
he'd entered the green-tiled room,
had seen her cut open in the O.R.,
the metastases studding the omentum,
thousands of tiny seeds, germinating.
Now he thought—she's done it again.
Her miraculous protoplasm, learning new
tricks, had fooled him.

                She had said—
you think you doctors are gods—to her
dearest brother. He would laugh, hold her,
and silently judge her chances, wondering
how soon they would close the lid on her
oblong box. He remembered the Egyptian way
of painting faces on coffins, or the eyes
wide, staring from the Djed-pillar,
a promise of eternity, those black-lined eyes
of Osiris that death couldn't close.

Prayer

"Birds build—but not I build; no, but strain
Time's eunuch, and not breed one work that wakes.
Mine, O thou lord of life, send my roots rain."
Gerard Manley Hopkins

Send rain, down to the dry bare bones of me,
    the tarsals planted in sand, no sage
    or mint or parsley will grow here, snails
    are sucked dry, leave frail shells
    in the dug garden's dirt, no flowers, no fronds;

Send rain, down to the deep bowl of my pelvis,
    barren red hollow, the empty sack
    sags now with age, the scarred yellow ovals
    discharge their eggs in irregular cycles,
    no longer linked so well to the moon;

Send rain, down to the restless quartered meat
    that thuds on my ribs, whose valves
    measure thin blood as it seeps through
    the pipes feeding desiccated organs,
    whose mortal work forms sludge;

Send rain, down to the small transparent curve,
    the opaque lens that filters dim light
    to the lustrous surface and on to dense
    convolutions of brain, the task of my sighted
    vitreous globes that turn in their padded cells;

Send rain, down to the knots and whorls
    where memory continues to pile its thick layers,
    sloughs surface, and roots reach into
    that grey ground where my neurons grow sparse
    and leached soil sprouts nothing new.

Send rain.

POETRY FROM ALICE JAMES BOOKS

The Calling Tom Absher   *Thirsty Day* Kathleen Aguero   *In the Mother Tongue* Catherine Anderson   *Personal Effects* Becker, Minton, Zuckerman   *Backtalk* Robin Becker   *Legacies* Suzanne Berger   *Disciplining the Devil's Country* Carole Borges   *Afterwards* Patricia Cumming   *Letter from an Outlying Province* Patricia Cumming   *Riding with the Fireworks* Anne Darr   *Chemo-Poet and Other Poems* Helene Davis   *Children of the Air* Theodore Deppe   *ThreeSome Poems* Dobbs, Gensler, Knies   *The Forked Rivers* Nancy Donegan   *33* Marjorie Fletcher   *US: Women* Marjorie Fletcher   *No One Took a Country from Me* Jacqueline Frank   *Forms of Conversion* Allison Funk   *Natural Affinities* Erica Funkhouser   *Rush to the Lake* Forrest Gander   *Without Roof* Kinereth Gensler   *Bonfire* Celia Gilbert   *Permanent Wave* Miriam Goodman   *Signal::Noise* Miriam Goodman   *To the Left of the Worshiper* Jeffrey Greene   *Romance and Capitalism at the Movies* Joan Joffe Hall   *Raw Honey* Marie Harris   *Making the House Fall Down* Beatrice Hawley   *The Old Chore* John Hildebidle   *Impossible Dreams* Pati Hill   *Robeson Street* Fanny Howe   *The Chicago Home* Linnea Johnson   *The Knot* Alice Jones   *From Room to Room* Jane Kenyon   *Streets after Rain* Elizabeth Knies   *Sleep Handbook* Nancy Lagomarsino   *The Secretary Parables* Nancy Lagomarsino   *Dreaming in Color* Ruth Lepson   *Falling Off the Roof* Karen Lindsey   *Temper* Margo Lockwood   *Black Dog* Margo Lockwood   *Rosetree* Sabra Loomis   *Shrunken Planets* Robert Louthan   *Sea Level* Suzanne Matson   *Animals* Alice Mattison   *The Common Life* David McKain   *The Canal Bed* Helena Minton   *Your Skin is a Country* Nora Mitchell   *Openers* Nina Nyhart   *French for Soldiers* Nina Nyhart   *Night Watches: Inventions on the Life of Maria Mitchell* Carole Oles   *Wolf Moon* Jean Pedrick   *Pride & Splendor* Jean Pedrick   *The Hardness Scale* Joyce Peseroff   *Before We Were Born* Carol Potter   *Lines Out* Rosamond Rosenmeier   *Curses* Lee Rudolph   *The Country Changes* Lee Rudolph   *Home Country* Cheryl Savageau   *Box Poems* Willa Schneberg   *Against That Time* Ron Schreiber   *Moving to a New Place* Ron Schreiber   *Contending with the Dark* Jeffrey Schwartz   *Changing Faces* Betsy Sholl   *Appalachian Winter* Betsy Sholl   *Rooms Overhead* Betsy Sholl   *From This Distance* Susan Snively   *Deception Pass* Sue Standing   *Infrequent Mysteries* Pamela Stewart   *Blue Holes* Laurel Trivelpiece   *Home. Deep. Blue. New and Selected Poems* Jean Valentine   *The River at Wolf* Jean Valentine   *The Trans-Siberian Railway* Cornelia Veenendaal   *Green Shaded Lamps* Cornelia Veenendaal   *Old Sheets* Larkin Warren   *Tamsen Donner: a woman's journey* Ruth Whitman   *Permanent Address* Ruth Whitman